27 Thou

Travis I. Sivart

27 Thoughts on Phrases That Changed My Life

Travis I. Sivart

Travis I. Sivart

27 Thoughts on Phrases That Changed My Life
27 Thoughts on Life Series, Book 3

Copyright © 2019 Travis I. Sivart

Cover Design by Travis I. Sivart
Edited by Tara Moeller

All rights reserved.

ISBN: 978-1-954214-45-3

Talk of the Tavern Publishing Group

Travis I. Sivart

Enjoying what you're reading?
Want some more for free?

Go to TravisSivart.com/work

Travis I. Sivart

Dedication

This book is for me, but dedicated to all those people, events, and life lessons that gave me what I needed to carry on.

27 Thoughts on Phrases That Changed My Life

Table of Contents

Dedication... ix

Introduction...xv

1. That's what average people do; I don't want to be average. 1

2. Argue your limitations, and they are yours. 3

3. Stress and tension are self-inflicted. 5

4. Today is the first day of the rest of your life. 7

5. If you don't choose your purpose, your life will never have one. 9

6. Just keep swimming.. 11

7. The right word can mean the world. 13

8. I've wrestled with reality for thirty-five years, Doc, and I'm happy to state I finally won out over it. 15

9. If I sit, my feet ache; if I walk, they rejoice. 17

10. Attitude: The difference between an ordeal and an adventure. 19

11. Never give up, never surrender! 21

12. Mourn not what you have lost, but rather, rejoice in what you have. 23

13. Whether you think you can or you can't, you're

right. 25

14. Here's to our vices; may we always choose them, but never be a slave to them! 27

15. A master has failed more than a beginner has tried. 29

16. Small blessings and silver linings are all we have some days. Learn to cherish them. 31

17. A smooth sea never made a skilled sailor. 33

18. Life isn't as serious as my mind makes it out to be. 35

19. What truly creates change is changing your own perspective and perception. 37

20. Expectation is the root of all heartache. 39

21. Approval comes with a price. Make sure you're willing to pay the latter before seeking the former. 41

22. A journey of a thousand miles begins with a single step. 43

23. It's the ride you remember, not the wait in line. ... 45

24. Success is measured not so much by the position that one has reached in life as by the obstacles he has to overcome while trying to succeed. 47

25. When you know you're dreaming, you can change and influence your dreams. Waking is no different. 49

26. Focus – Commitment – Pure Will 51

27. Admit your own worth; to yourself, and to others. 53

About the Author.. 57

Travis I. Sivart

Introduction

Like everyone, I've gone through my personal, difficult moments in life. These are phrases that inspired me in those challenging times. These phrases have been on Post-It Notes on my monitor, on 3x5 cards tucked in my sun visor, scrawled on my dry erase boards, or written a dozen times in various steno pads as I transferred notes from one to the other.

Some of the wisdom is from others, famous sayings that have lasted the ages. Others are from movies, just key quotes that stuck in my head when I needed that tidbit of advice. And still others are from my own experiences and are my words.

I often analyze my situation and look for a succinct answer that sums the issues up nicely; or a reminder to make sure I don't get myself into the same problem again in the future.

These ideas are nothing new. They've been around since we began inventing philosophy. Use what helps you and don't worry about the rest. I hope these 27 phrases can help inspire and caution you as effectively as they have me.

Travis I. Sivart

1. That's what average people do; I don't want to be average.

Travis I. Sivart

Average people make up most of our population, that's why they're average. These everyday folks who wake up, go to work, come home, watch TV and check their computers, eat dinner, and go to bed are the core of our society and I have immense respect for them.

But, I don't want to be like them. I tried it, and it didn't work out. It was like committing suicide of my mind and personality. I tried very hard, but just couldn't do it. I failed at being normal.

Instead, I dream wild dreams, then pursue them. I take risks that sensible people wouldn't consider. I learn new skills just to do something one time. I stay up too late to experience something, and go to work dead tired the next day. I don't have the best car, newest phone, or get new living room furniture every couple of years. But I've gone to Europe on a shoestring, painted every wall in my house a different color, dress in a tux and tails to go out for fast food, and wrote books about whatever strikes my fancy.

I live my dreams and fantasies, which is not what the average person does. But, I don't want to be average.

Travis I. Sivart

2. Argue your limitations, and they are yours.

Richard Bach, Illusions

This is from a book I read in my mid-teens, and it changed my view of life. It was a serious, honest-to-God, life-changing moment. I've reread the book every couple of years and remind myself of what I knew as a teen, and perhaps even learn something new as my perspective changes.

We all have limits, and it's good to know them. But that doesn't mean we can't push our boundaries and comfort zones. Arguing for your limitations is one sure way to ensure defeat before you even start. Self-imposed restrictions are one sure way to never make your dreams come true. Don't do that to yourself.

Travis I. Sivart

3. Stress and tension are self-inflicted.
Travis I. Sivart

I worry. Most people do. I sometimes get into a cycle of thinking about situations or circumstances so that I get tension headaches. This isn't a pressure put on me by anyone else. I do it to myself.

Then one day I realized my mind creates that stress and tension. I consciously recognized this and set it aside. It comes back occasionally, and I have to do it again.

It isn't easy to do this, but by being aware that you are causing yourself harm, you can stop this cycle. Some folks cut themselves, and this is an emotional and mental way of doing the same thing.

Face your issues, take care of what you can, plan for the rest. But don't dwell on the things you cannot change at this very moment. Stop cutting yourself.

Travis I. Sivart

4. Today is the first day of the rest of your life.

Charles Dederich

A phrase made popular in the 1970s, though I'm sure the concept was around long before ol' Chuck came up with it as a slogan.

We wake up every morning to face a new day, and every new day is another chance to succeed. It can be a fresh beginning, if you allow it to be. More than that, you have to put your mental foot down and decide that it's a clean slate, any hardships or failures in the past can be let go of, and you can move forward.

Don't be your own anchor to hold yourself back. Don't let your past failures decide that you cannot have future success. Start new, now, today.

Travis I. Sivart

5. If you don't choose your purpose, your life will never have one.

Travis I. Sivart

Many people seek a purpose in their life. The secret is that you get to decide what this is. This was said well in the Classic Billy Crystal and Jack Palance comedy, City Slickers.

In a scene, Billy's character was frustrated and Jack's character asked, "Do you know what the meaning of life is?"

Billy shook his head, and Jack held up a gloved finger and said, "One thing, this."

"Your finger?" Billy asked.

"No, it's one thing." Jack growled.

"What is it?" Billy shouted.

"That's up to you to decide." Jack answered.

Maybe I'm paraphrasing the conversation, but that's the gist of it. You decide what your purpose is, what your goal will be, and what's important to you. Then you make your life have purpose and meaning with that one thing.

Travis I. Sivart

6. Just keep swimming.

Dory, Finding Nemo

A classic kid's movie from Pixar, but it held a gem of wisdom from the absent-minded, tag-along, comedy-relief friend, Dory. She even sang a song about it, "Just Keep Swimming."

In life, you can't give up, or not move forward, and expect to have things come to you. Though that may work occasionally, it isn't a sure thing. The only sure way to continue to have a life be interesting and to succeed is to keep moving forward. I reflect on this idea in a couple of other thoughts in this book.

It's important to not give up. Giving up is the only guaranteed way to fail.

Travis I. Sivart

7. The right word can mean the world.
Travis I. Sivart

This is a quote I put in the very first book I published. As an author, it holds a lot of truth. In the literal sense, many words can mean the world. Globe, Earth, biosphere, planet, etc. In the non-literal way, which is the manner I mean for this phrase, just a single word can change someone's life.

I'm usually an upbeat fellow, but one day in my teens, I was walking along the sidewalk in sunny Florida with my head down and my hands shoved in my pockets. I was in a foul mood. I passed a middle-aged woman. Usually I'd make eye contact, smile, and give a pleasantry. That day, I was in no mood to deal with anyone. As we passed, she said, "Hello."

That single word struck me. I muttered hello back to her. Then I walked with my head up. I smiled. I pulled my hands out of my pockets and put my shoulders back. Her single word changed my day and my mood.

My point is, a single word from you can change someone's day. A phone call or message can improve their week. A conversation can change their entire outlook. Don't ignore this ability to influence others in a positive way. And don't use it to create negative results.

Travis I. Sivart

8. I've wrestled with reality for thirty-five years, Doc, and I'm happy to state I finally won out over it.
Elwood P. Dowd, Harvey

Reality can be a bitch. Life can be hard. But you have to let it be that way to you. You have to set your mind to it to make this happens.

Of course, you have to also set your mind to let life be fun. To make reality what you want, a positive environment, you have to wrestle with it. Shape it and make it what you want. This takes time and effort. Don't let it bear you down. Fight for your reality to be something you want to live in.

Choose to surround yourself with things that make you happy. Do things that make you feel good and appreciate the things you have.

Travis I. Sivart

9. If I sit, my feet ache; if I walk, they rejoice.

Travis I. Sivart

I first said this in my mid-teens. Most folks didn't understand what I meant by it, though. I will explain it to you now. If I stay still in life and don't move forward, I feel like I'm missing something. And I am, I'm missing success and adventure in life.

When I move forward in life, and attempt to do things, I find I'm happy. I look forward to what the next day brings. I crave to create something. This may be a story, a painting, a good meal, or just to clean and organize my home.

Any way it goes, moving forward creates a positive reaction in me, but doing nothing makes me ache inside for something else.

Travis I. Sivart

10. Attitude: The difference between an ordeal and an adventure.
Travis I. Sivart

Life throws challenges at us. If we're smart and/or motivated, then most of them are self-created. But either way, we face trials almost every day. And it's our attitude as we deal with them that decides if they're troublesome ordeals, or exciting adventures.

If you stress and suffer every time something comes up, life becomes a tribulation. You spend so much time worrying about what you are facing; you don't bother to see past it to what you can have once you beat it.

Most things that happen to us that make us upset or frustrated…if it happened in a movie or TV show you were watching, you'd know the person will overcome it and get the reward waiting on the other side. You sit forward in your chair, excited, wanting to know how your favorite character will win out over whatever it is they're facing.

Why not do that in your own life? Smile, roll up your sleeves, take charge, and put the work in, knowing you'll get something worthwhile once it's passed.

Travis I. Sivart

11. Never give up, never surrender!
Galaxy Quest

Galaxy Quest was a great movie, full of exciting challenges and funny lines. But the one line that stuck with me is the catchphrase of the crew: "Never give up, never surrender!"

It means that, well, just what it says. Don't lay down and give up. Don't let life beat you. Anything can be overcome and beat if you just don't give up. It's pretty simple.

I've used this as a mantra when things are particularly tough for me. I find myself muttering it as I drive, reminding myself that I can't be beat if I don't give up, if I don't surrender. It's helped me grit my teeth and push forward, and through, anything I was dealing with.

Travis I. Sivart

12. Mourn not what you have lost, but rather, rejoice in what you have.

Travis I. Sivart

Life is ever changing. One of my many stepfathers used to say, "Nothing is constant, except change." Life is full of things and people that come and go. You'll lose things in this life, that's a fact.

I've lost friends and family to the ebb and flow of life. Some have died, some just fade away. It makes me sad until I realize I still have others around me that care. And by focusing on what I have, it makes me realize the value of what I still retain, and I'm grateful for that.

I've had many jobs, homes, and belongings. I've lost more than what I have, but I have what I need. The things that are gone were wonderful when I had them, but to disregard what I currently have to mourn what I no longer can have, seems just silly and harmful to my mental state.

I still remember these people and things from time to time, but I do it with a wistful smile, enjoying the memory. Then I go and enjoy what I have around me right now.

Travis I. Sivart

13. Whether you think you can or you can't, you're right.

Henry Ford

Henry Ford, the man known for making the first mass-produced automobile, as well as being a prosperous businessman, was also a wise man. He coined this phrase, meaning that you decide if you can succeed before you even start.

It's your own belief in yourself that ultimately decides if you flourish or fail. If you move forward expecting to bomb, you will. It's pretty much a guarantee.

A can-do attitude paves the way to achieving whatever it is you're attempting to do.

14. Here's to our vices; may we choose them, and never be a slave to them!

Travis I. Sivart

I enjoy a drink, a pipe or cigar, a good movie, and the occasional video game. I love to take a day and waste it sitting on the couch, with my feet up and cats purring in my lap. But none of these things will ever be a stumbling block to me succeeding.

I don't have addictions, though they have reared their ugly head on occasion. I don't allow my vices to have so much control over me I can't put them down, walk away, and do something I want to do.

Travis I. Sivart

15. A master has failed more times than a beginner has tried.

Hindi Saying

We're all beginners at some point. We may have a talent for one particular thing, but it doesn't mean we're great at it, just that we have a knack for it.

Many people give up when a certain skill doesn't come easy. I don't know if our society is more self-entitled now—as many would claim—or if it's always been that way, but you can't just pick up a new thing and be a master of it. You have to work, and work long and hard, to become truly great at a thing.

Popular culture says you're a master once you have done something for ten-thousand hours. That's over a year's worth of work, if you're doing it twenty-four hours a day. But we rarely work over eight hours a day, five days a week. That means it takes over five years of full-time work to become a master. Now, apply that logic to a skill that others would call a hobby, like painting, music, or writing. These things would take much more than five years, because we rarely partake of our hobbies as frequently or at the same length as we do work.

If you love something, though, work at it. Practice it. Devote time and energy to it. You will become skilled in time; sometimes slowly, sometimes with an epiphany that lets you grow in leaps and bounds. The bottom line is to keep trying until you are a master, then try some more.

16. Small blessings and silver linings are all we have some days. Learn to cherish them.

Travis I. Sivart

Life can be harsh, come at you quick, and overwhelm you with the sheer mass of challenges. To help keep your psychological equilibrium and emotional balance, appreciating the small things in life is essential.

Every day, we have dozens of small successes; getting out of bed, hygiene routines, a laugh with a friend, seeing something that makes you smile or giggle, a delicious treat, and any of the other things we see, do, or experience on a daily basis.

Remembering these is important. Appreciating them is even more important. It's so easy to only recall the bad or annoying things at the end of the day. But we must pull the good things to the front, and move on from what brings us down.

Make a practice of doing this. When you remember something from your day, your brain produces the same chemicals—good or bad—that were produced when you first experienced the event. If you ate something nasty during the day, and something wonderful later, which flavor would you rather experience again once you're home?

The same goes for remembering.

Travis I. Sivart

17. A smooth sea never made a skilled sailor.

Franklin D. Roosevelt

Adversity builds character is another way of saying this. Which isn't completely true; but for most folks that fight their way through problems and come out the other side, they gain a new way of looking at things.

By facing problems, issues, challenges, trials, and tribulations in life, it teaches us to see beyond that and keep our eye on what we're trying to accomplish.

Also, by facing these challenges, you build your skill set. This may be a physical skill set associated with an activity (such as painting, repairing cars, or any number of things) or it may be less tangible and take form in a social skill set, such as when you deal with difficult people.

The bottom line is that facing issues and overcoming them allows you to grow and become more skilled in ways that only experience can provide.

Travis I. Sivart

18. Life isn't as serious as my mind makes it out to be.

Travis I. Sivart

I sometimes need to stop, take a deep breath, and remind myself to calm down and everything will be ok. On occasion, I'll compare life to a movie and encourage myself to see it from the frame of reference of the audience, knowing it will end well, and once this scene has passed, it'll no longer matter.

This isn't to say I should have a completely flippant attitude about what's happening in my world. But instead, to not allow the drama of a single moment to cloud my view of the larger picture of my life.

Life isn't a joke, but you'll enjoy it more if you learn to laugh more often than you worry.

19. What truly creates change is changing your perspective and perception.

Travis I. Sivart

Changing your point of view is mind expanding. Seeing the world through someone else's eyes is something that can alter your life and how you treat people forever.

Your perspective is limited, and your perception of your perspective further categorizes, boxes, labels, defines, and confines what you see, hear, and experience in any form. When you look at something, let's use a house, for example, you see it and experience it. If you move further away, you can see its surroundings and how those affect it. If you move closer, you can see details showing care or abuse. If you walk all the way around the house, you can see the yard, neighbors, the back door, and so many other things you may not have seen from the porch. And if you move inside it, it's a whole other world.

This is the same for people, places, events, experiences, or anything else. Changing your perspective allows you a different, and unique, view of whatever it is you're observing. Changing your perception allows you to see it from the inside, exposing so much more than you can see from the outside. Knowledge and understanding are the key to change.

Travis I. Sivart

20. Expectation is the root of all heartache.

William Shakespeare

This is a simple truth. If you have a predesignated concept of what will happen, you've already set yourself up to be disappointed.

There's a difference between working towards a goal with likely results, and having expectations with no acceptance of the possibility of something else happening.

This is true when it comes to projects, relationships, work, or anything else. Leave possibilities open and it'll pleasantly surprise you when things turn out differently than you thought, rather than being heartbroken when they don't turn out the way you expected.

21. Approval comes at a price. Make sure you're willing to pay the latter before seeking the former.

Travis I. Sivart

If you run around hoping to gain other people's approval, that means you're doing something for them rather than yourself. It costs you something to gain another person's appreciation, gratitude, or endorsement.

It may be your time while you try to do things that please the other person (whether that's your boss, a friend, a family member, your significant other, or just some stranger), or it could be your resources, your pride, or even other friendships.

Before you try to gain someone's favor by doing whatever it is you think they want, or what would please them; consider the cost you'll pay for that.

22. A journey of a thousand miles begins with a single step.

Lao Tzu

Dory said it well, "Just keep swimming." In Galaxy Quest they said, "Never give up, never surrender!" It's an ageless saying, and for some folks (like myself) a life philosophy.

This boils down to "you can't get anywhere without moving forward." To achieve anything you MUST move, keep moving, one foot in front of the other, don't stop, don't give up, and keep on keeping on.

It's such a common saying in so many forms that it's often just assimilated into our cultural surroundings and we lose sight of the value of the wisdom the thought holds.

To recap; you can't succeed in anything without doing something.

Travis I. Sivart

23. It's the ride you remember, not the wait in line.

Travis I. Sivart

When my son was just a wee lad of seven or eight years of age, I took him to Disney World. We were standing in a long and winding line; it was hot, and he was waiting patiently. I don't know if he overheard someone complaining, but he suddenly said, "When you get home from the park, it's the ride you remember, not the wait in line."

In life, we often find ourselves impatiently waiting for the next thing to happen. First, enjoy that wait as a break between the peaks and valleys of life. Second, at the end of your life—when you look back across the years—you aren't going to remember the slow times, the waiting, the downtime. Instead, you'll remember the ride. The peaks and valleys of life.

So when in a holding pattern, relax. It's ok. You'll have plenty of rides to remember.

Travis I. Sivart

24. Success is measured not so much by the position that one has reached in life as by the obstacles he has to overcome while trying to succeed.
Booker T. Washington

I've known many successful people in life, and in almost every instance, the more they overcame to reach where they were...was matched by the level of respect they garnered from others around them.

A marathon runner who's in their twilight years and has overcome a stroke will often gain more attention than a young man in his twenties who runs the same marathon. The same can be applied to someone who made their way through college or university by earning money or scholarships rather than someone who was given money and didn't have to hold a job while earning their degree.

If you want to measure your success, look at how much you've done, how much you've worked, overcome, or fought to get where you are. It stands out and shows passion and drive above and beyond what another may have who had to do less to get to the same place.

Travis I. Sivart

25. When you know you're dreaming, you can change and influence your dreams. Waking is no different.
Travis I. Sivart

This is a tough concept to wrap your head around, similar to not taking life too seriously because no one gets out alive. Or becoming so wrapped up in a problem that you can't see past it, and you end up suffering because you won't let yourself do anything else.

When you're dreaming and being chased by a monster, if you can realize that you're dreaming, you can make choices that you couldn't otherwise. You can choose to fight, to fly, to turn the monster into a bunny. Real life can be very similar, and you can choose how to perceive things, and realize all things are temporary and can be changed through your own will and effort.

26. Focus – Commitment – Pure Will
John Wick

This is a philosophy introduced in an action movie, and it is a perfect recipe for succeeding in life. The main character does things no other man can, through these three things.

Focus. Giving your full attention to something allows you to analyze it in ways that partial attention does not. It lets you look at things, finding other options, ways, and methods of handling it. Or it allows you to fully commit to the task.

Commitment. You're much less likely to complete any task if you're not committed to succeeding at it. Going "all in" gives you effort and energy to overcoming obstacles, finding that creative drive, or making whatever it is to do what you want to do.

Pure Will. Not giving up is key to succeeding in any task, no matter how small or monumental. Having the willpower to work out, lose weight, write a book, get that job, finish that course, or whatever it is you're doing is how you see things through when all your other inspirations have faded.

27. Admit your own worth; to yourself, and to others.

Travis I. Sivart

So many people, especially creative people, don't recognize their own worth, skills, or ability. They're often shy, self-demeaning, or just don't want to brag.

There's a difference between confidence and being arrogant and tooting your own horn. The first step is admitting to yourself that what you offer is worth having. You have value, and others appreciate it.

Many times, though, people are so busy with their own lives that they fail to recognize the value others offer. There's nothing wrong with being proud of yourself, as long as it isn't at the expense of others. There's never a need to elevate yourself by putting others down.

But you should always feel comfortable talking about your own achievements and worth when appropriate.

Enjoying what you're reading?
Want some more for free?

Go to TravisSivart.com/work

Travis I. Sivart

About the Author

Travis I. Sivart is a prolific author of Fantasy, Science Fiction, Social DIY, and more. He's created The Traverse Reality, a shared universe that connects his cyberpunk, fantasy, and steampunk worlds, and writes characters who feel real to his readers.

You can sometimes find him live-streaming the writing and editing of his latest project from his home in Central Virginia, surrounded by too many cats.

You can find Travis at www.TravisISivart.com.

Travis I. Sivart

If you enjoyed this book...

Please let others know by reviewing it on Amazon or Goodreads, and let others know your thoughts!

Other books by Travis I. Sivart:

27 Thoughts on Enjoying Life

Travis I. Sivart draws on his lifetime of helping other to offer his personal guidelines for enjoying life. This book offers twenty-seven thoughts on helping create happiness in your personal life, success in your professional life, and even manage depression on a daily basis by suggesting ways to improve and maintain your mental, physical, and emotional well-being.

Steampunk For Simpletons: A Fun Primer For Folks Who Aren't Sure What Steampunk Is All About

A primer followed by a guided tour through the world of steampunk, from the basics such as where to go and what to do, to the aesthetic of the arts within steampunk.

Journal of a Stranger

The thoughts, ideas, philosophies, and inspirations of a time traveling adventurer. Delving into the psychology of man, life's eternal questions, burning passions, and the quirky pseudo-science of his mind, and more.

27 Thoughts about Steampunk

Travis I. Sivart draws on his passion of steampunk as an aesthetic and a hobby to offer his personal insights for helping others to begin delving into this fascinating culture and genre. This book offers twenty-seven thoughts on the basic questions and concepts that often crop up when someone is beginning to explore this incredible movement.

Travis I. Sivart

Travis I. Sivart